A Garden
Instruct

To Henry and Daisy

Follow these hints,

you will be the best

Gardeners

11 x

A Gardener's Little Instruction Book

Violet Wood

HarperCollins*Publishers*

HarperCollins*Publishers*
77–85 Fulham Palace Road,
Hammersmith, London W6 8JB

www.**fire**and**water**.com

First published by Thorsons 1996
Published by HarperCollins*Publishers* 1999

3 5 7 9 10 8 6 4

© Violet Wood 1996

Violet Wood asserts the moral right
to be identified as the author of this work.

Illustrations by Mike Gordon

A catalogue record for this book
is available from the British Library

ISBN 0 7225 3907 X

Printed and bound in Great Britain by
Martins the Printers Ltd, Berwick upon Tweed

In memory of my grandmother
who first inspired me to garden

Introduction

Gardening is probably one of the most popular leisure pursuits there is. For some it's a passion, even perhaps an obsession; for others it's a pleasant way to idle away a sunny afternoon.

For me gardening is therapy. I am rarely more at peace than when working in my garden. Life seems to be problem-free when you're concentrating on weeding, digging or planting. And, oh, the joy of gathering armfuls of flowers or vegetables.

I first became interested in gardening as a small child when I stayed with my grandparents deep in the heart of the Garden of England – Kent. My grandmother never read gardening books, but she seemed to be a fount of knowledge and her garden was a mass of blooms, fruits and vegetables. Some of her tips I've passed on here, others I've gathered over the years from fellow gardeners. I've also thrown in a sprinkling of gardening thoughts to amuse and inspire you.

If you, like me, enjoy gardening, then I hope you will enjoy this little book.

- Everyone needs a garden of their own

- Look at weeding as one of life's therapies

- Don't throw snails over your garden wall

- It's fine to dream, but work at making your dream garden a reality

- Sow and transplant only with a waxing, never a waning, moon

- Get your lawn-mower overhauled *before* the grass-cutting season begins

- Order your seeds in the winter, from the comfort of your armchair

Make sure you have some Japanese anemones – they are a wonderful standby, blooming from late summer through to autumn, and the white version makes a splendid background plant for bright colours

Don't procrastinate, rather get ahead

* Nothing looks nicer than a collection of nicely weathered terracotta pots

* Keep your shed tidy – that way you'll be able to find what you need

* Aquilegias are perfect perennials for a low maintenance garden, with both glorious flowers and attractive foliage

- Don't be disappointed if all your seeds don't germinate

- Listen to your plants, as well as talking to them

- Avoid falling in the pond

- Be patient

- Plant heliotrope for its sensational cherry-pie perfume

- For reliable autumn colour, plant the deciduous varieties of cotoneaster and berberis

- Don't worry about mistakes – that's how you learn

Nasturtiums make a bright showing of red, yellow and orange, but like a poor soil, so do not feed them

❀ Be sure to keep a patch of nettles – butterflies love them

❀ Plant marigolds next to your carrots – root fly hate the smell

❀ Do gardening jobs as soon as you see they need doing

🌼 Keep a garden notebook, because you won't remember where everything is planted, or when you planted it

🌼 Sow some hardy annuals to edge a border

🌼 Always carry secateurs – you're bound to need them

❁ Learn botanical names

❁ Remember that a bright sunny morning may be just that, so don't put off tasks that have to be done and find it's raining

❁ Keep greenfly off your roses by underplanting with clumps of chives

✿ Take a nap occasionally

✿ Plant hollyhocks, sunflowers, mulleins, foxgloves, delphiniums and giant dahlias at the back of borders

✿ Check you have everything you need before you set off to the bottom of the garden

🌸 Plant a buddleia and watch the butterflies dance

🌸 Be satisfied with your accomplishments

🌸 Do some gentle backward stretching to compensate for too much bending

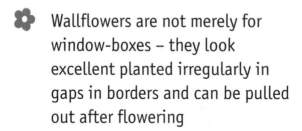

Wallflowers are not merely for window-boxes – they look excellent planted irregularly in gaps in borders and can be pulled out after flowering

The watching and the waiting teach important lessons for life

Always grow a few pots of good summer annuals such as nicotianas – they make wonderful space-fillers when other plants have died down

❀ If you have a shady border, the best plants are monkshood, Japanese anemone, astrantia, astilbe, bergenia, brunnera, hosta, lamium, aquilegia and Solomon's seal

❀ Be generous with your cuttings

❀ Wear a hat when it's hot

❁ Look out for Gertrude Jekyll's books – she was one of the twentieth century's most influential gardeners

❁ Take time to wonder

❁ Listen to the weather forecast – frosts can strike unexpectedly

❁ Plant penstemons to freshen up parched borders – they are ideal late summer perennials

❁ Understand when to prune and when not to prune

❁ Tend your compost heap with love

✿ To brighten up a dull patch of garden border, sprinkle poppy seeds over it in the spring

✿ The experience of growing things is healing

❀ Nothing shakes off depression quicker than a little time spent working in the garden

❀ Don't be lazy about staking your plants

❀ Even in the depths of winter, there are signs of life to come

🌼 *Always* put your gardening shoes on, even if you think you'll keep to the pathways – you never do

🌼 Save your empty loo rolls – they make great planters for starting off sweet peas

🌼 Save your empty plastic bottles – cut in half they make superb individual cloches

❁ Water your seedlings with care and watch them grow

❁ Planting a garden brings untold happiness

❁ Don't grumble about the autumn clear-up – debris and bonfires are part of the process and have their own charm

🌼 Birds are wonderful companions when you're digging

🌼 Every day is the opportunity to create something beautiful

🌼 Take care of your soil

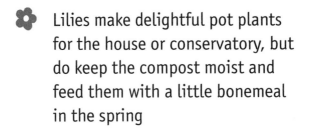 Lilies make delightful pot plants for the house or conservatory, but do keep the compost moist and feed them with a little bonemeal in the spring

Liquid seaweed is a marvellous tonic for your plants

🌸 Learn to love rain – it is as
necessary as the sun

🌸 Remember the saying 'Sow one
seed for the rook, one for the
crow, one to die and one to grow'

🌸 Find out from neighbouring
gardeners what grows well locally

❀ Don't disturb the worms

❀ Save your autumn leaves – once rotted down (separate from your compost) they make a superb mulch for spring weeds

❀ Don't sow seed when the ground is too cold

🌼 Don't overdo it

🌼 Rotate your vegetables to prevent the soil from becoming exhausted

🌼 Don't wash your face in the bird bath

🌼 Water gardens should not look like a lawn of duckweed

🌸 Remember that Nature is never idle, even if you are

🌸 Avoid gnomes

❀ Never plant Leyland cypress if you want to be taken seriously

❀ The best hardy annuals for summer colour include pot marigold, candytuft, clarkia, cornflower, godetia, larkspur, mignonette, love-in-a-mist, poppies and sweet peas

Don't ruin your garden with badly chosen furniture

Do not plant a tree too near to the house

Grow some borage with your strawberries – they make excellent companions

✿ The common foxglove stimulates growth of neighbouring plants and helps disease resistance

✿ Sow turnip seed thickly if you want to get rid of couch grass

✿ You can always try *eating* ground elder – use the young leaves as for spinach

Grow Mexican marigolds (*Tagetes signata pumila*) to control ground elder or horsetail

🌸 Don't worry about your plants
spilling over lawn edges – tidiness
is not a virtue

🌸 Leave your classy labels dangling
so everyone can see you've been
to the right nursery

🌸 Mix old-fashioned shrub roses
with repeat-flowering ones

- Don't always follow the advice of old herbals, particularly those which suggest naked seed-sowing

- Join the Royal Horticultural Society

- If you really want to impress, join the Soil Association and the Henry Doubleday Research Association

✿ Tea leaves are an excellent mulch for camellias and roses

✿ Avoid Pampas grass

✿ Grow herbs everywhere – not only will you have a constant supply for cooking, but they also help keep pests away from your fruit and vegetables

Dahlias seem to prefer their own bed or corner rather than being mixed in with other flowers

- Weedkiller is only permissible on paths and drives

- Avoid crazy paving – york stone is better

- Climbing plants are essential to cover brick or stonework

❀ Don't forget the edible flowers –
pot marigolds, nasturtiums,
violets, borage

❀ If you want to gather roses, mind
the thorns

❀ Avoid gimmicky gadgets – they're
not necessary

🌼 Make dandelion wine (that's one way of getting rid of them) but don't drink too much of it

🌼 Never go on holiday in summer – you might miss something

🌼 Water tubs and containers daily in hot weather

Don't trust anyone else in the garden – they're bound to think your prize plants are weeds and pull them up

- Remember that the young think gardening is the passion of the middle-aged because they have grown too old for sex

- Keep off the garden in frost and snow

- Never give up

🌼 There is always the right place for the right plant

🌼 It's no good lying in bed thinking of everything to be done

🌼 Your garden is a reflection of your state of mind

A mulch is a weeder's best friend

Good soil, like good looks, isn't something you're born with

Grow giant vegetables just for fun

You can't necessarily trust the experts, but you can your instincts

- Frost and snow will rid you of some of the garden's enemies

- The secret of abundance is careful husbandry

- Make your flower beds large and your borders wide

Before you light a bonfire, check there isn't a hedgehog hibernating in it

Don't envy others their gardens – think of all the work that goes into them

Lean on your hoe from time to time

Every gardener knows something you don't, so learn from others

Accept help – you cannot do it alone

Remember, one year's weeds, seven years' seeds

❁ Other people's tools work only in other people's gardens

❁ Even a window-box reveals something about its owner

❁ Watch your feet when using a scythe

❁ Do not line your garden pond with turquoise PVC – it is not a public swimming bath

❁ When putting in new plants, don't press down too heavily – use finger pressure

✿ If a plant looks dead, give it the benefit of the doubt for a few more weeks – it will probably start to perk up

✿ Don't say there isn't time – you can always find time if you want to

✿ You need a little optimism

- Break the rules and let vegetables go to seed occasionally – flowers and seedheads can be stunning

- Don't be afraid to move a plant to a different position

- Use urns and jardinières to make a focal point in your garden

❀ Plant annuals like poached egg plant (*Limnanthes douglasii*) between your herbs and vegetables

❀ Keep plants clear of aphids by companion planting or use pirimicarb, which will not harm other more beneficial insects

❀ Watch your fingers when using loppers

- Remember what that famous gardener Gertrude Jekyll said – 'A garden is far more than just a collection of plants'

- Don't stand underneath your hanging baskets when watering them

- Summer savory will keep onion fly from your onions

❊ Visit the Royal National Rose Society Garden in Hertfordshire – it is one of the best places to see roses

❊ Pray for rain

❊ While most herbs grow easily, parsley is notoriously difficult to get started

❀ Trim your lawn edges to set off both lawn and borders

❀ Grow mint, sage, thyme or rosemary alongside your cabbages

❀ Face facts – the only way to stop cats digging in your borders is not to have any borders

❀ Don't let your garden turn you into a snob – four apple trees do not an orchard make

❀ If you cannot arrange for someone to water your container plants whilst you are away on holiday, move them into the shade after a good soaking

🌸 Find out whether plants prefer sun or shade

🌸 Shroud your carrots, celery and cabbages in finely spun fleece to protect against root flies

✿ Employ a gardener – but take the credit for his handiwork

✿ When dead-heading roses, also remove the suckers at the base

✿ If you need some rain, light the barbecue

❀ Gardening is about sharing the problems as well as the remedies

❀ Do not have turf laid during a hosepipe ban

❀ If you want to avoid pesticides, use derris or insecticidal soap

- Grow low-growing annuals like ageratums, busy lizzies and gazanias on sunny window-sills

- Be *very* sure before you eat any mushrooms from your garden

- Colour-theme your containers rather than having a mass of different colours

Grow vegetables such as ruby chard and red cabbage in the flower border for visual as well as edible benefit

- Embrace diversity – a wide range of crops and varieties will help combat pests and diseases

- Borage leaves are essential for Pimms

- Listen to Gardeners' Question Time

Walk around the garden early in the morning and at twilight to spot any problems – undesirable pests are more likely to be lurking then

 Nasturtiums are a good companion for apples

Buy a copy of *Gardens of England and Wales* each year – it lists over 3,000 private gardens to visit

Use a small onion hoe to weed densely planted beds

❀ Remember that it's snobs who tell you that you should only grow old-fashioned roses

❀ Always water plants in the evening during hot weather

❀ Plant a scented shrub by your door to greet visitors

❁ Try a coir dust based compost instead of peat

❁ Don't expect your sundial to take account of Summer Time

❁ Plant your garden to look like Vita Sackville-West's

Think in terms of feeding the soil, rather than feeding the plant

Hostas are excellent as marginal plants beside a pond or stream

Make sure that you garden with love

✿ If you need a little inspiration, buy a gardening magazine or send off for some catalogues

✿ Take cuttings of tender plants like penstemons or hebes as an insurance against losses in a bad winter

❁ Make sure your sprinkler is facing the right way when you turn it on

❁ Choose plants with pretty foliage as well as flowers, like hepaticas

❁ Remember that many common garden plants are poisonous, e.g. rhododendrons, laburnum, yew

❀ Buy the very best tools you can afford, stainless steel if possible

❀ Use annuals to fill in any gaps in herbaceous borders

❀ Site your garden pool where there is plenty of sunshine

❀ Never put off picking courgettes until tomorrow

❀ Don't devote your life to cultivating a garden and then hang a permanent washing line across the middle of it

❀ Tend your garden and you will find peace of mind

🌼 Remember that life began in
a garden

🌼 Keep a gardening diary to
compare what you did in
previous years

🌼 Wipe your tools with an oily cloth
after use for maximum life

❀ Remember that you get second chances with gardening – there's always the next season

❀ Plant shows are an excellent opportunity to pick up useful tips from the growers

❀ Rotted down newspaper, finely shredded, can help suppress weeds

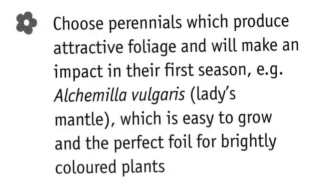 Choose perennials which produce attractive foliage and will make an impact in their first season, e.g. *Alchemilla vulgaris* (lady's mantle), which is easy to grow and the perfect foil for brightly coloured plants

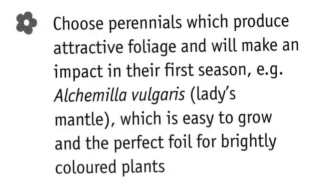 If your garden is immaculate, get a sign saying 'Beware of the Gardener'

- Use a barrier of ash or sharp grit to deter slugs from eating perennials

- Send away for seed catalogues each year – they are full of ideas and gardening advice

- Always clean pots and seed trays carefully with garden disinfectant

🌸 Jerusalem artichokes make an excellent windbreak in the vegetable garden

🌸 Be sure to earth up potatoes to prevent tubers from becoming green and poisonous

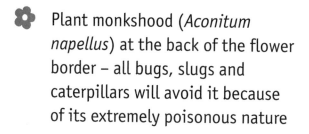

Plant monkshood (*Aconitum napellus*) at the back of the flower border – all bugs, slugs and caterpillars will avoid it because of its extremely poisonous nature

Do not place tender plants in an east-facing situation – the early morning sun in winter will cause damage

- Always deadhead roses with secateurs and cut back to a leaf or bud

- Leave filled watering cans to warm up in the greenhouse so that seedlings don't have the shock of cold water

- Plant runner and french beans in the most sheltered part of the vegetable garden

Feed roses with a slow-release fertilizer like bonemeal in the spring

In dry weather remember that a good soak for plants and containers is better than a drizzle every day

Discuss your garden with friends and neighbours and exchange cuttings

- Do not get a dog if you value your lawn

- Don't light a bonfire too close to the trees

- Trim the roots and leaves of leeks before planting in an oversized hole, then fill the hole with water

🌸 Remember that work done in the spring will cut out twice as much in the summer

🌸 Plant a clove of garlic by each rose to ward off vampires – and greenfly

🌸 Remember that weeds are opportunists

❁ Never despair if your garden is bordered by overhanging trees – plant hawthorn and hazel, dog roses, honeysuckle and clematis

❁ The art of good mulching is to block out weeds, encourage the roots of plants and retain moisture

🌼 Do not plant merely for dreamy summers

🌼 Always sow seeds thinly – crowded seedlings never grow well

🌼 Mix dust-like seeds with a pinch of dry silver sand to make sowing easier

❁ Grow red and green salad bowl lettuce at the front of the flower border

❁ It does not do to rush things in the garden – a shrub may take 10 years to flower, a tree 100 years to reach maturity

❁ Water pots and trays from below after sowing

✿ Don't be fooled into thinking it's all as quick and easy as on *Gardener's World*

✿ In a drought, use your bath water on the garden – but fish the soap out first

✿ Read, look, think and plan

✿ Know your weeds

✿ Most shrubs should be pruned immediately after flowering

✿ Cover fruit bushes with netting to keep the birds away

✿ Remember to turn seed-trays on window-sills round each day

- Hoe on dry days

- Don't scorn the onion family – it is a source of spectacular beauty and terrific for companion planting

- Try growing sweetcorn at the back of the flower border

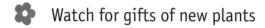

🌸 Watch for gifts of new plants

🌸 When tidying the garden for winter, don't cut everything down. A layer of dead growth protects from frosts

Do not waste water. Instead:

i) incorporate organic matter into the soil to act as a sponge

ii) grow plants close together so that the leaves join in a protective umbrella

iii) apply a mulch to stop evaporation

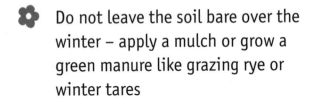 Do not leave the soil bare over the winter – apply a mulch or grow a green manure like grazing rye or winter tares

Seek out old varieties of vegetables – they are less dependent on chemical input and will also have better flavour

Armchair gardening is OK too

❁ Save yourself some backache –
don't double-dig and leave the
soil micro-organisms in peace

❁ Though it's nice to cut some
flowers for inside, leave some
in the garden

❁ Keep a log of interesting birds or
animals that visit your garden

❀ Always plant fresh bulbs in containers, transferring old ones, once the foliage has died down, to the garden

❀ Wear gloves at all times if you want your hands to look attractive

❀ Keep off the soil in winter or you will compact it

In the vegetable garden, cover some areas with polythene or plastic cloches to warm the soil prior to planting

When sowing, remember that little and often is best – that way you can keep a succession of plants going

Prune so that it looks as if you haven't touched the plant

Don't mow your lawn too short – a little growth protects the roots during drought and hot sun

There is nothing nicer than propagating a few plants to give as presents

Make your garden a haven for wildlife and let nature solve the problem of pests

Don't leave things to chance – plant supports should be put in the border before the plants have grown too tall

If soil sticks to your boots in spring, wait until it is drier before forking over

Remember that rain can damage your soil by leaching out nutrients

Remember the Chinese proverb 'He who plants a garden, plants happiness'

Low-growing hedges such as box or lavender make a charming edge for flower or vegetable beds

✿ Gardening is an exercise in letting go

✿ Learn to live in the garden if you want to live off it

✿ Don't be put off by the smell of blood, bone and fishmeal – they are organic and do your plants a power of good

Plant pennyroyal to ward off ants

Be in touch with what the garden wants by 'listening' to it

Don't be fooled – April and May can be treacherous months

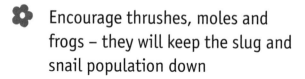 Encourage thrushes, moles and frogs – they will keep the slug and snail population down

Encourage thrushes, moles and frogs – they will keep the slug and snail population down

If the lush green leaves on your camellias turn yellow, give them a tonic of iron sequestrene

- If plain green shoots start appearing on your variegated plants, cut them off at the base

- Remember the summer-flowering bulbs – lilies, gladioli and alliums

- Raze your chives to the ground and you will get another crop

Don't scoff at hardy annuals –
they are a cheap and cheerful
means of providing colour

Don't be afraid to experiment
with pips – lemon, orange and
grapefruit pips can all grow into
handsome trees

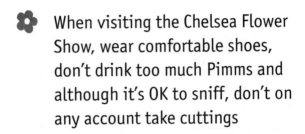 When visiting the Chelsea Flower Show, wear comfortable shoes, don't drink too much Pimms and although it's OK to sniff, don't on any account take cuttings

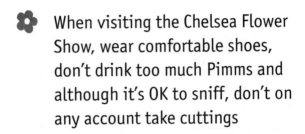 Don't get too carried away at Chelsea and order plants inappropriate for your garden

But do buy some seeds at Chelsea

❀ Dead-head seedpods of daffodils to give stronger bulbs

❀ Remember that pot plants on window-sills need a lighter mixture of soil

❀ French marigolds attract useful insects, while the smell repels those you don't want

❀ In order to work your garden, get to know the soil, the aspect and the micro-climate

❀ It always helps to know what other gardeners have done

❀ Plant up hanging baskets but leave inside until they look mature and colourful

Pests, diseases and weeds have no scruples – they appear in the best of gardens

Leave the digging and aerating to the worms – they pull down the goodness from your mulch into the topsoil

Become fond of the hoe

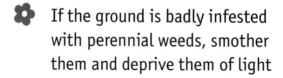 If the ground is badly infested with perennial weeds, smother them and deprive them of light

Another use for old tights – cut them into strips to make soft, strong ties for below flower spikes

🌸 Remember that your garden reveals a lot of clues about your personality

🌸 Regular dead-heading encourages more flowers

🌸 Encourage hoverflies to act as nature's pest controllers by planting *Convolvulus tricolor* and other flowers

✿ Always check sowing instructions on seed packets

✿ If you have trouble with slugs and snails, good flowers to plant are bleeding heart (*Dicentra spectabilis*), sedum, aquilegia and forget-me-nots (*Myosotis*) – they seem to resist them

❁ Always harden off young plants raised in a greenhouse before planting out

❁ Don't be afraid about not being overly clean and tidy – hedgehogs, beetles and spiders love a pile of rubbish and will help fight pests

When digging, don't automatically reach for the spade – a fork does a better job and is kinder to worms

When visiting a garden centre, never buy a plant which is dry at the roots

Catalogues are crucial for the long winter nights

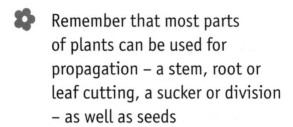 Remember that most parts of plants can be used for propagation – a stem, root or leaf cutting, a sucker or division – as well as seeds

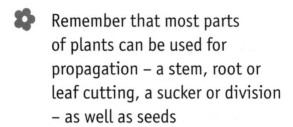 When planting out in dry conditions, always water the hole before you put the plant in, mulch with organic matter and then water thoroughly

❁ You will always feel better in the garden

❁ Choose trees that are even more fascinating in winter than in summer, like *Sorbus hupehensis*, which has ferny green leaves, autumn colour and pink-tinged white berries

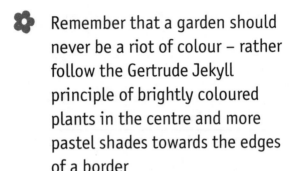 Remember that a garden should never be a riot of colour – rather follow the Gertrude Jekyll principle of brightly coloured plants in the centre and more pastel shades towards the edges of a border

There are always ideas to copy or adapt, so visit as many gardens as possible

❀ Collecting plants is like collecting anything – make sure that you keep it under control

❀ Remember the saying about ivy – 'The first year it sleeps, the second year it creeps, the third year it leaps'

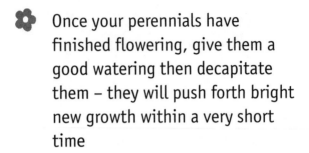 Once your perennials have finished flowering, give them a good watering then decapitate them – they will push forth bright new growth within a very short time

Day lilies (*Hemerocallis*) will settle anywhere and last for years, and are one of the best herbaceous perennials

✿ Split your herbaceous plants every three years or so

✿ Good summer flowers for containers in a hot dry spot, or on a roof garden, are osteospermums, mesembryanthemums and Californian poppies (*Eschscholtzia californica*)

- Grow mignonette for its beautiful perfume

- Scatter grit around your alpine plants – it enhances their appearance and also ensures that they are not damaged by rain splashing soil on to them

- A garden is never finished

✿ For a beautiful display in spring, plant less familiar bulbs like snake's head fritillaries (*Fritillaria meleagris*)

✿ For winter flowers and fragrance, plant Chinese viburnums, particularly *Viburnum farreri* or the large flowered *Viburnum bodnantense*

❀ A beautiful garden is like a beautiful painting – it does not reveal itself all at once

❀ Vegetables can be ornamental as well as tasty

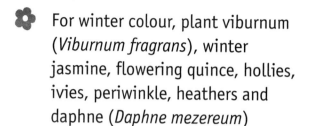 For winter colour, plant viburnum (*Viburnum fragrans*), winter jasmine, flowering quince, hollies, ivies, periwinkle, heathers and daphne (*Daphne mezereum*)

Don't get depressed when you return from a holiday to find your garden has become unruly

❁ Miracles happen

❁ Share your produce

❁ Truly, you reap what you sow